THE MOST BEAUTIFUL SONGS

FOR EASY CLASSICAL PIANO

5 OF THE BEST ARRANGED BY PHILLIP KEVEREN

Cover photo courtesy Library of Congress, Prints & Photographs Division,
photograph by Carol M. Highsmith

— PIANO LEVEL —
INTERMEDIATE

ISBN 978-1-4950-9416-3

HAL•LEONARD®
7777 W. BLUEMOUND RD. P.O. BOX 13819 MILWAUKEE, WI 53213

Visit Hal Leonard Online at
www.halleonard.com

Visit Phillip at
www.phillipkeveren.com

PREFACE

The popular songs in this collection have stood the test of time. Like a well-built home with, as they say, "good bones" that can be decorated in lots of different ways, these tunes can and have been arranged in many musical styles over the decades.

Using classical compositional devices, these beautiful songs have been developed into character pieces for piano solo.

Musically yours,

Phillip Keveren

BIOGRAPHY

Phillip Keveren, a multi-talented keyboard artist and composer, has composed original works in a variety of genres from piano solo to symphonic orchestra. Mr. Keveren gives frequent concerts and workshops for teachers and their students in the United States, Canada, Europe, and Asia. Mr. Keveren holds a B.M. in composition from California State University Northridge and a M.M. in composition from the University of Southern California.

CONTENTS

AND I LOVE YOU SO

Words and Music by
DON McLEAN
Arranged by Phillip Keveren

Passionately (♩ = 108-112)

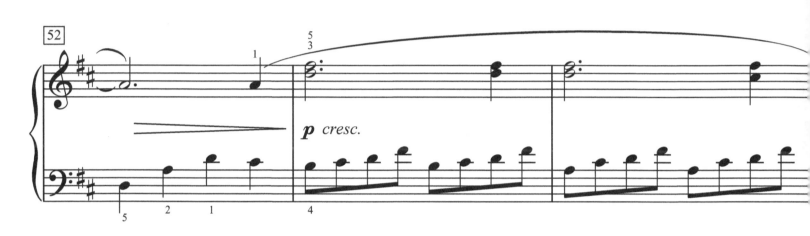

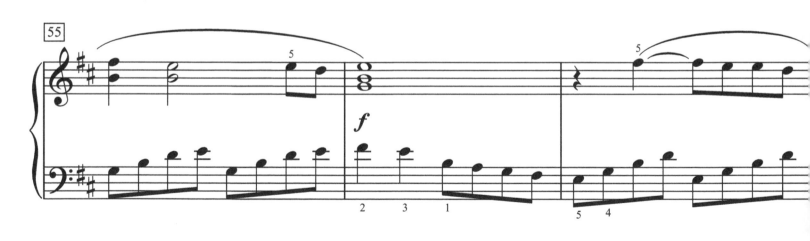

DREAM

Words and Music by
JOHNNY MERCER
Arranged by Phillip Keveren

Like a watercolor (♩ = 116)

EBB TIDE

Music by ROBERT MAXWELL
Lyric by CARL SIGMAN
Arranged by Phillip Keveren

Serenely, with freedom ($\quarternote$ = c. 60)

Moving forward (♩ = 88)

Tempo I ($\quarternote$ = c. 60)

molto rit.

FLY ME TO THE MOON
(In Other Words)

Words and Music by
BART HOWARD
Arranged by Phillip Kevere

HERE'S THAT RAINY DAY

Words by JOHNNY BURKE
Music by JIMMY VAN HEUSEN

Slowly, with rubato (♩ = c. 80)

I WILL WAIT FOR YOU

from THE UMBRELLAS OF CHERBOURG

Music by MICHEL LEGRAND
Original French Text by JACQUES DEMY
English Words by NORMAN GIMBEL
Arranged by Phillip Keveren

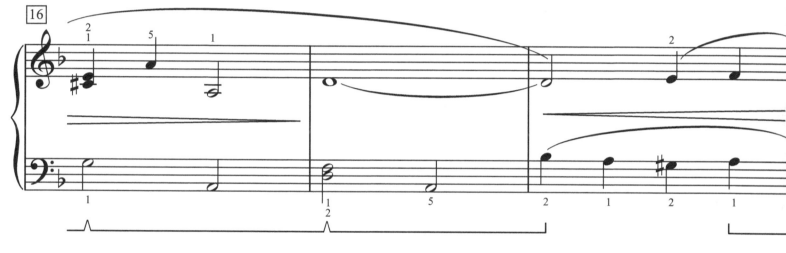

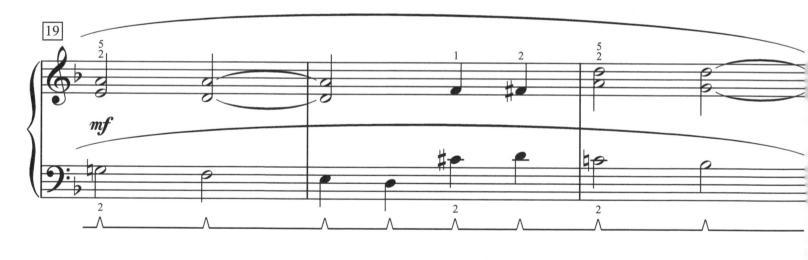

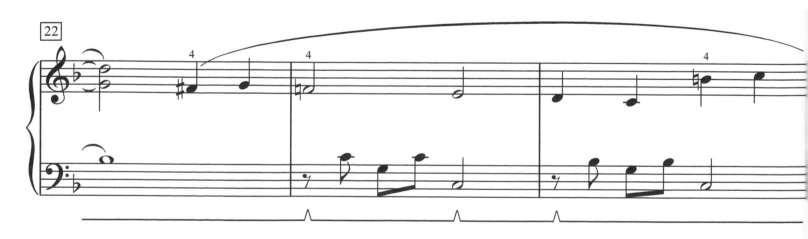

IN THE WEE SMALL HOURS OF THE MORNING

Words by BOB HILLIARD
Music by DAVID MANN

LONGER

Words and Music by
DAN FOGELBERG
Arranged by Phillip Keveren

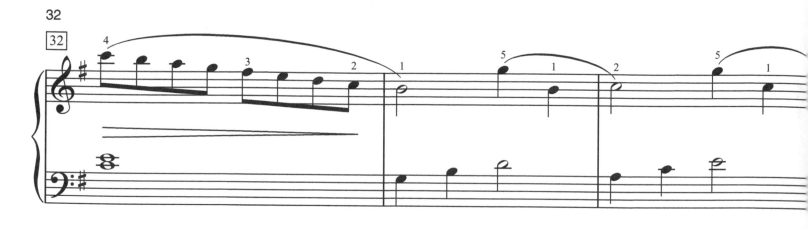

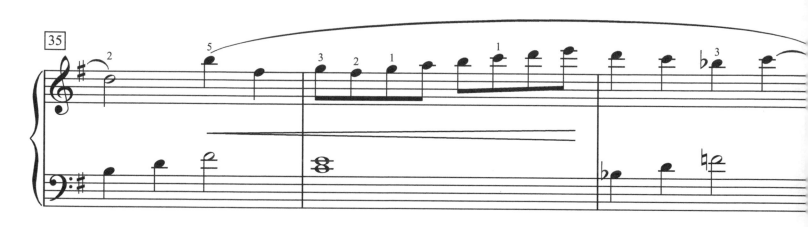

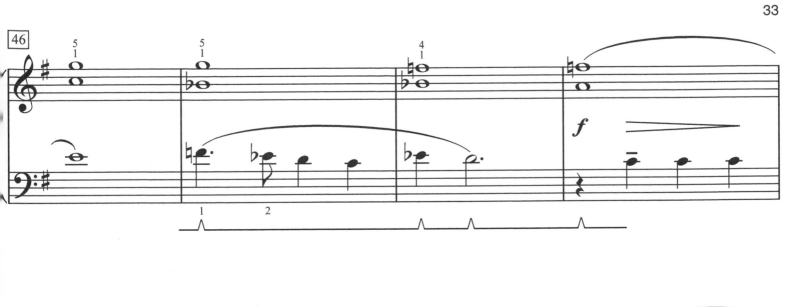

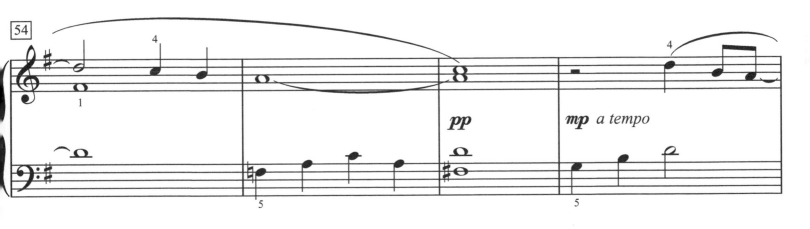

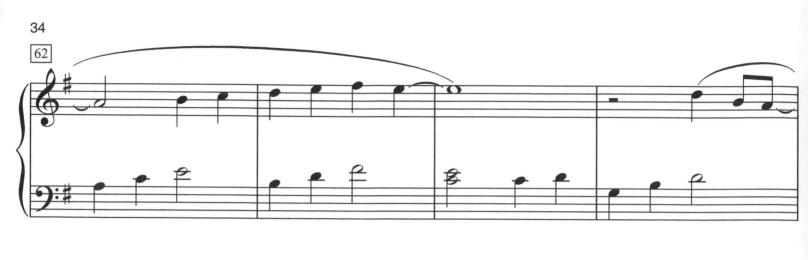

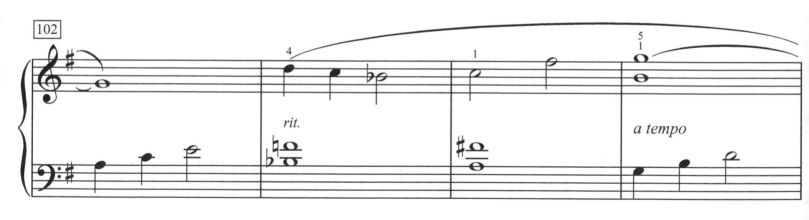

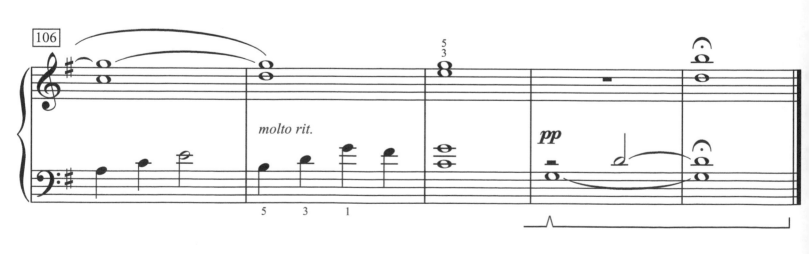

MY CHERIE AMOUR

Words and Music by STEVIE WONDER,
SYLVIA MOY and HENRY COSBY
Arranged by Phillip Keveren

OH, WHAT A BEAUTIFUL MORNIN'

from OKLAHOMA!

Lyric by OSCAR HAMMERSTEIN II
Music by RICHARD RODGERS
Arranged by Phillip Keveren

42

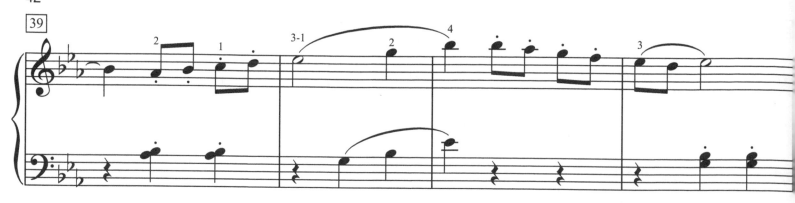

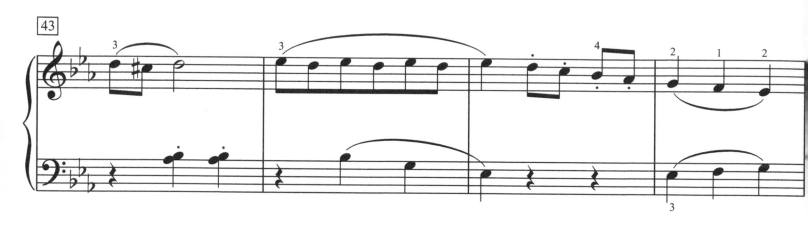

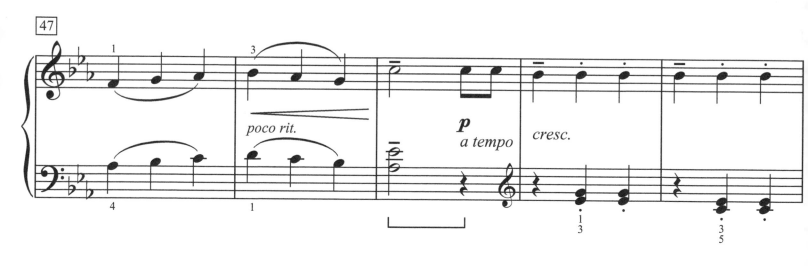

September Song

from the Musical Play KNICKERBOCKER HOLIDAY
(Introduction quoting Debussy's "The Girl with the Flaxen Hair")

Words by MAXWELL ANDERSON
Music by KURT WEILL
Arranged by Phillip Keveren

46

SOMEWHERE, MY LOVE

Lara's Theme from DOCTOR ZHIVAGO
(with Tchaikovsky's "The Sleeping Beauty Waltz")

Lyric by PAUL FRANCIS WEBSTER
Music by MAURICE JARRE
Arranged by Phillip Keveren

48

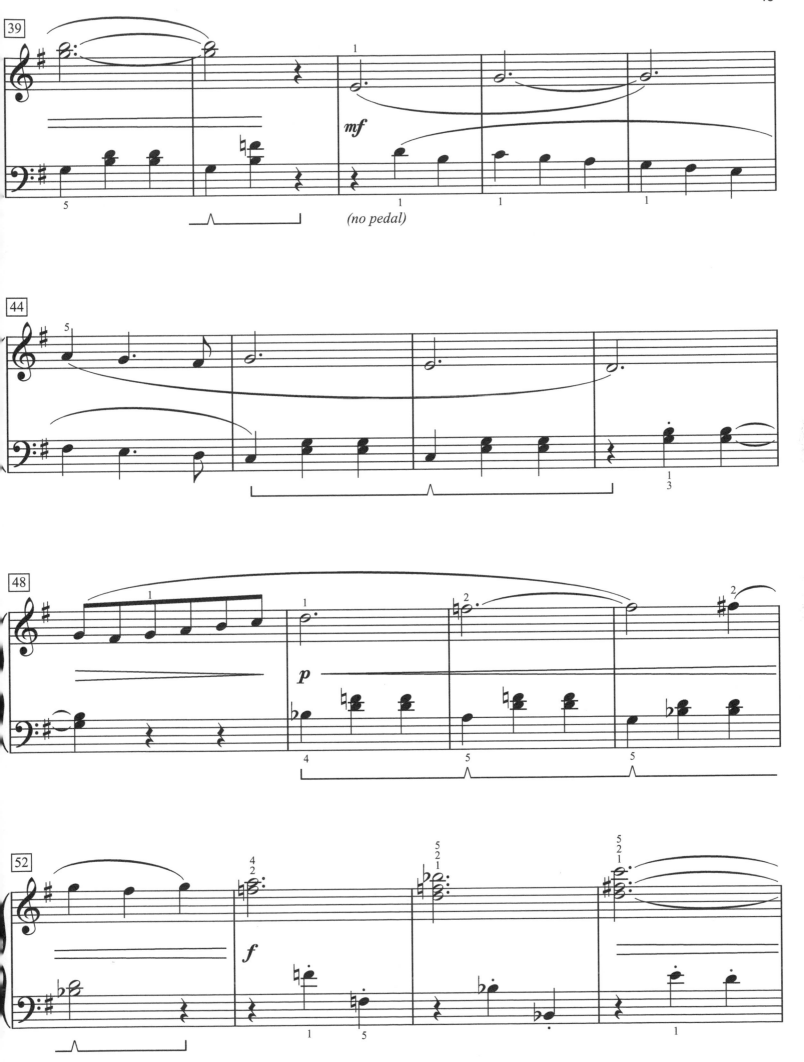

(no pedal)

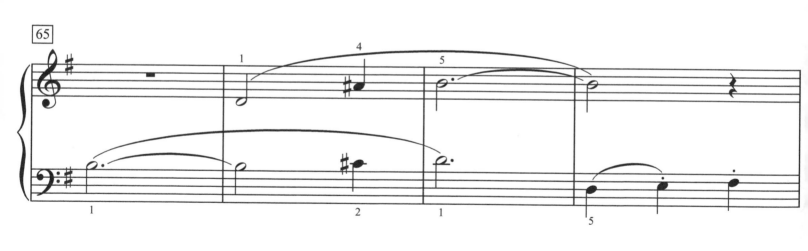

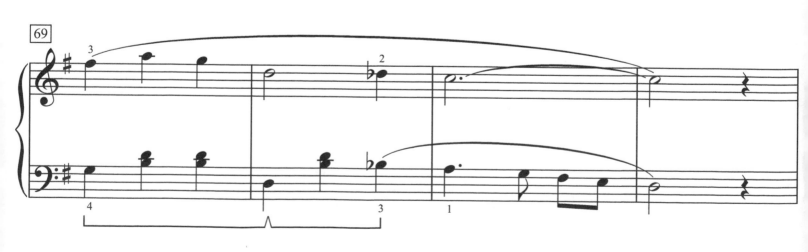

UNCHAINED MELODY

Lyric by HY ZARET
Music by ALEX NORTH
Arranged by Phillip Keveren

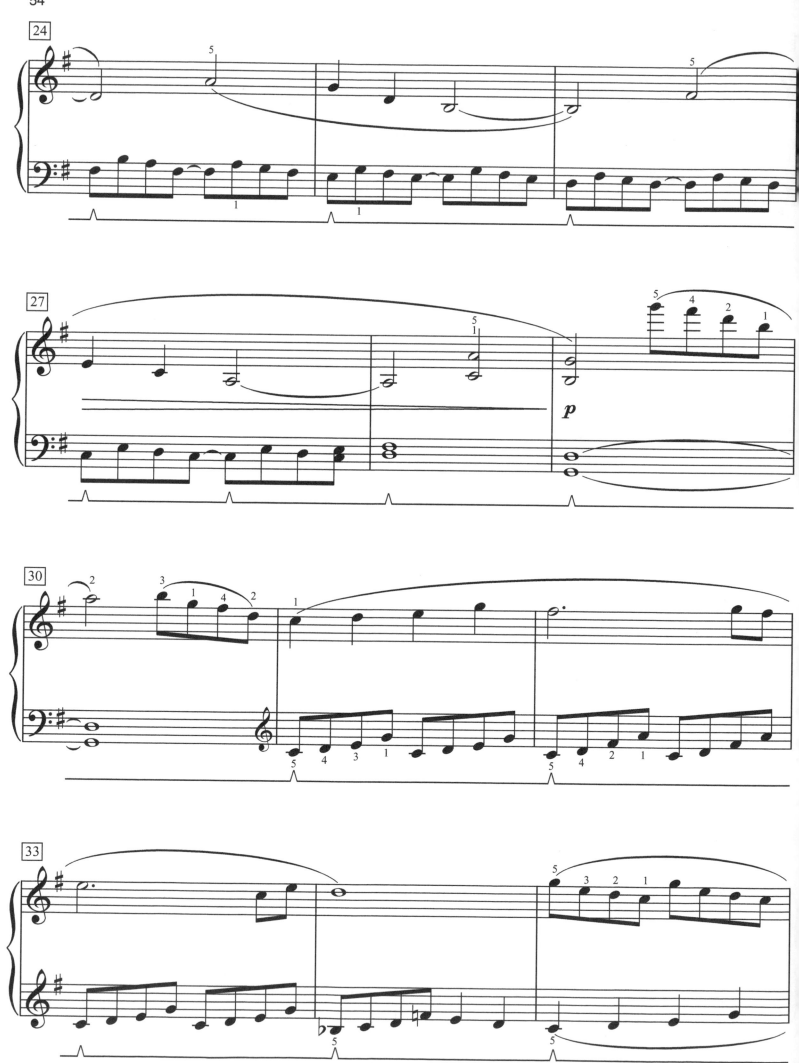

WILLOW WEEP FOR ME

Words and Music by
ANN RONELL

Gently swaying (♩. = 58)

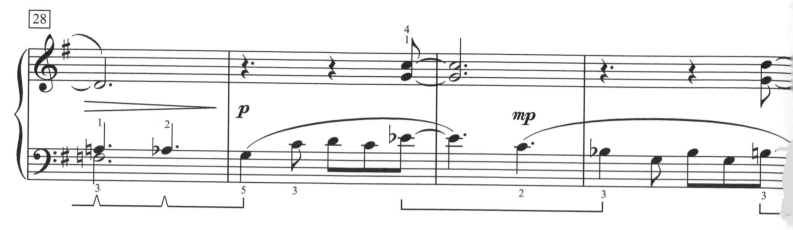

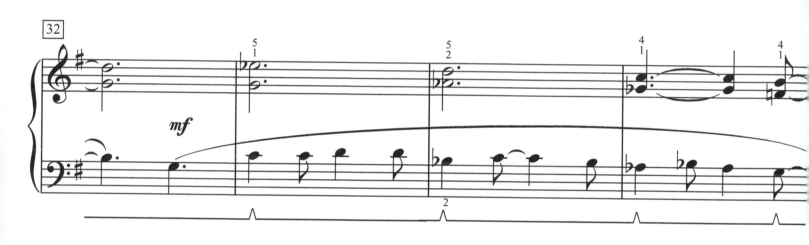

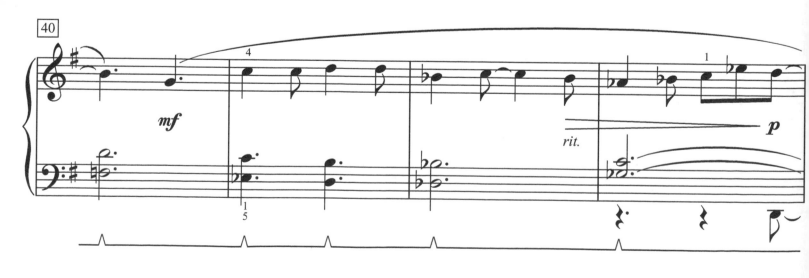

STRANGERS IN THE NIGHT

adapted from A MAN COULD GET KILLED
(Inspired by Schumann's "Little Piece," Op. 68, No. 5)

Words by CHARLES SINGLETON
and EDDIE SNYDER
Music by BERT KAEMPFERT
Arranged by Phillip Keveren